AUTORE

Luigi Manes (18 luglio 1966) ha già pubblicato due volumi insieme ad altri autori, "Italia 43-45 – I mezzi delle unità cobelligeranti" (2018 - Mattioli 1885) con Paolo Crippa e "Carri armati Sherman in Sicilia" (2018 - Edizioni Ardite) con Lorenzo Bovi. Ha inoltre realizzato vari articoli per la rivista di modellismo militare "Steel Art" e per il sito "ModellismoPiù". Da sempre interessato alla storia della Seconda Guerra Mondiale, nutre una grande passione per il carro armato medio Sherman, sia dal punto di vista storico sia da quello tecnologico.

AUTHOR

Luigi Manes (18 luglio 1966) has already published two books with other authors, "Italy 43-45 – AFV's and MV's of co-belligerent units" (Mattioli 1885 – 2018) with Paolo Crippa and "Carri armati Sherman in Sicilia" (2018 – Edizioni Ardite) with Lorenzo Bovi. He has written various articles, both for the military modeling magazine "Steel Art" and the website "ModellismoPiù". Always interested in the history of Second World War, he has a great passion for the Sherman medium tank from an historical and technological point of view.

PUBLISHING'S NOTES

None of unpublished images or text of our book may be reproduced in any format without the expressed written permission of Luca Cristini Editore (already Soldiershop.com) when not indicate as marked with license creative commons 3.0 or 4.0. Luca Cristini Editore has made every reasonable effort to locate, contact and acknowledge rights holders and to correctly apply terms and conditions to Content.

Every effort has been made to trace the copyright of all the photographs. If there are unintentional omissions, please contact the publisher in writing at: info@soldiershop.com, who will correct all subsequent editions.

Our trademark: Luca Cristini Editore©, and the names of our series & brand: Soldiershop, Witness to war, Museum book, Bookmoon, Soldiers&Weapons, Battlefield, War in colour, Historical Biographies, Darwin's view, Fabula, Altrastoria, Italia Storica Ebook, Witness To History, Soldiers, Weapons & Uniforms, Storia etc. are herein @ by Luca Cristini Editore.

LICENSES COMMONS

This book may utilize part of material marked with license creative commons 3.0 or 4.0 (CC BY 4.0), (CC BY-ND 4.0), (CC BY-SA 4.0) or (CC0 1.0). We give appropriate attribution credit and indicate if change were made in the acknowledgments field. Our WTW books series utilize only fonts licensed under the SIL Open Font License or other free use license.

ACKNOWLEDGMENTS

The aim of this book is to give the reader a photographic record of the Sherman tank variants employed by Allied Armies in the European Theater of Operations. I would like to express my sincere thanks to Luca Cristini for his constant support during the preparation of the volume and to my friends Mario Bentivoglio, Paolo Crippa and Andrea Sala, for having encouraged me to publish this work.

Luigi Manes

For a complete list of Soldiershop titles please contact Luca Cristini Editore on our website: www.soldiershop.com or www.cristinieditore.com. E-mail: info@soldiershop.com

Title: **THE SHERMAN MEDIUM TANK in the European Theater of Operations** Code.: WTW-004 ENG
By Luigi Manes.
ISBN code: 978-88-93274630 First edition June 2019
English text Nr. of images: 133 layout: 177,8x254mm Cover & Art Design: Luca S. Cristini

WITNESS TO WAR (SOLDIERSHOP) is a trademark of Luca Cristini Editore, via Orio, 35/4 - 24050 Zanica (BG) ITALY.

WITNESS TO WAR

THE SHERMAN MEDIUM TANK

IN THE EUROPEAN THEATER OF OPERATIONS

PHOTOS & IMAGES FROM WORLD WARTIME ARCHIVES

LUIGI MANES

ENGLISH TEXT

BOOKS TO COLLECT

CONTENTS

THE SHERMAN MEDIUM TANK IN THE ETO .... Pag. 5

The US Army Shermans .... Pag. 8

The English Shermans .... Pag. 57

The Canadian Shermans .... Pag. 75

The Czechoslovak Shermans .... Pag. 85

The French Shermans .... Pag. 86

The Polish Shermans .... Pag. 93

Bibliography .... Pag. 98

▲ Manifesto propagandistico statunitense - 2a Guerra Mondiale (U.S. WW2 Propaganda Poster)

THE SHERMAN MEDIUM TANK IN THE EUROPEAN THEATER OF OPERATIONS

The official U.S. Army armor doctrine of the early World War II period stressed the use of armored fighting vehicles for exploitations. Tanks were to be employed primarily as a maneuvering force in support of infantry offensive operations.

To engage and defeat concentrations of enemy armor was the task of the *Tank Destroyer Battalions*, equipped with towed anti-tank guns and self-propelled tank destroyers. The American Sherman, which could run over long distances without major mechanical failure, was a medium tank perfectly suited to deep penetration tactics.

The U.S. armored units that landed in Normandy were equipped mostly with M4 and M4A1 radial engine-powered Shermans, all with 75 mm guns. The M3 gun mounted on the Sherman was still capable of destroying the Panzerkampfwagen IV but the appearance of heavier German tanks like the Tiger and the Panther dramatically changed the situation.

It must be said that tank-versus-tank fighting wasn't the most common form of combat in World War II. Tanks were often involved in actions against "soft" targets such as enemy infantry, artilleries and other non-armored vehicles.

However, when the Panther was encountered in quantities in Normandy, it became clear that the 75 mm armed Sherman was inadequate in tank battles. The Panther could easily defeat the Sherman from normal combat ranges of 1,000 yards. On the contrary, the main armament of the allied tank could not pierce the thick and well sloped frontal armor of the Panther, even at short ranges. In order to overcome the problem, the British tried to improve the firepower of their tanks. The A30 Challenger, based on the Cromwell tank, would have had the powerful 17-pounder gun (76.2 mm) which boasted excellent anti-tank performance.

Even if the Challenger was put into production, the British were convinced that the Sherman was a better mount for the 17-pounder. The result of the conversion, carried out on M4 and M4A4 variants, was the Firefly, by the D-Day the most effective of all Shermans.

These tanks were supplied with three types of ammunition: APC (Armour Piercing Capped), APCBC (Armour Piercing Capped Ballistic Capped), and HE (High Explosive). At 1,000 yards, the standard APCBC round could pierce 5.1 inches of homogeneous armor at 30° degrees. In August 1944, the new APDS (Armour Piercing Discarding Sabot) round appeared. Although rather inaccurate, it was capable of penetrating the glacis of the heavy Tiger II German tank at 1,500 yards.

The Americans refused to equip their Shermans with the 17-pounder because the 76 mm gun and a powerful 90 mm gun were already in development. The M1A1 76 mm gun on the new M4A1 (76) w and M4A3 (76) w Sherman tanks could theoretically knock out the Panther at 500 yards using the new tungsten carbide cored T4 High Velocity Armor Piercing ammunition against its frontal armor.

A small batch of M4A1 (76)s was first delivered to the 2nd and 3rd Armored Divisions in late July 1944 but many U.S. tank commanders were reluctant to replace their old Shermans as the high explosive projectile fired from the 76 mm gun carried less filler than the high explosive round for the 75 mm gun. If the U.S. Army had been hesitant to adopt the 76 mm Sherman in the summer of 1944, this attitude had completely changed by January 1945. To provide added high explosive firepower to armored units, the Americans developed the M4 (105) and the M4A3 (105) assault guns.

In the closing months of the conflict in Europe, every U.S. Tank Battalion would have had six of them. The British need for howitzer tanks based on the Sherman was significantly lower.

U.S. official documents state that the British Army was supplied with 593 M4(105)s but it seems that none were used on northwestern European battlefields. The Three Rivers Regiment of the 1st Canadian Armoured Brigade was one of the Commonwealth units in the theater that had a limited number of M4(105)s, as demonstrated by some photographs taken shortly after the war.

The Ford-engined M4A3 (75) in its modernized version which was to be the basic model of the Sherman used by U.S. Army for many years, not only received three types of armament (the M3 75mm gun, the M1A1 76 mm gun and the M4 105mm howitzer) but was also converted to the M4A3E2, a heavily armored assault tank which had a new cast turret with 6 inch thick walls. The protection was improved by welding additional armor plates over the hull front and on the sides and by adopting a new heavier differential cover.

The M4A3E2 (254 units built) was fitted with the 75 mm gun, better suited for infantry support but later, about 100 of these assault tanks were re-armed with the 76 mm gun.

They were employed in Europe by the U.S. Army since the Fall of 1944 and at least one of them was supplied to the 2e Régiment de Chasseurs d'Afrique of the 1st French Armored Division. The argument over the role of tanks in U.S. armored units raged until events in the battlefields proved that success or failure hinged on the ability to skillfully employ a combination of infantry and tanks in combat operations.

In 1942, the American armored division was essentially intended for the exploitation of breakthroughs. According to the U.S. Army *Tables of Organization&Equipment*, the unit had two armored regiments, each with three tank battalions but only a single armored infantry regiment. The 1942 division was definitely tank centered as it possessed 232 medium tanks and 158 light tanks. In September 1943 a new lighter configuration with three tank battalions and three armored infantry battalions was introduced. Each tank battalion had three companies of Sherman medium tanks and one company of Stuarts light tanks.

The 1943 division therefore showed a higher ratio of armored infantry to tanks, having only 186 Shermans and 77 Stuarts. Thirteen of the fifteen U.S. armored divisions and nearly all the separate U.S. tank battalions that entered combat in the European Theater of Operations followed the light pattern, with the exception of the 2nd and 3rd Armored Divisions that retained the old, heavy, configuration.

Due to the limited utility of Stuarts, most U.S. light tank battalions were essentially re-equipped with Sherman medium tanks. The Free French Army fielded three armored divisions, organized on American lines. Each of them received 165 Shermans, mainly M4A2s (75)s and M4A4s (75)s, models that the Americans gave to their allies in Europe.

The 2nd French Armored Division, attached to U.S. Third Army, landed in Normandy about two months after the D-Day. Although entirely equipped with M4A2s, it nonetheless had some M4 (105)s. After having suffered various losses in the summer of 1944, this division obtained a small number of Sherman types generally reserved to American formations: M4 (75) s s and M4A1 (75)s (usually assigned to artillery and reconnaissance units) as well as M4A3s (with 75 mm or 76 mm guns and very few with 105 mm howitzer).

The 1st and the 5th French Armored Divisions both originally had a mixture of M4A2s and M4A4s. During the course of the European campaign, tank losses were replaced with other M4A4s but also with M4A1 (76)s.

A few 105 mm Shermans were allocated to the 2e Régiment de Cuirassiers that was part of the 1st French Armored Division. It is proven fact that at least two regiments of the 5th French Armored Division received some M4A1 (75)s and a handful of M4A1 (76)s before the end of the war. British armor doctrine was more focused on the defeat of German tank units than the American example.

Every British armoured brigade was constituted with three armoured regiments which basically were battalion-sized formations. The armoured regiment possessed three squadrons (A, B, C) and a HQ. The Regimental HQ was usually provided with 4 tanks (3 of them were observation posts with wooden dummy guns) and each squadron had 15 medium tanks on 5 troops (HQ Troop comprised and provided with observation posts tanks); a structure of 4 troops, 4 tanks was later adopted.

Apart from the specialized armored units in the 79th Armoured Division, the British Army deployed six Armoured Brigades equipped with Shermans in the European Theater of Operations. The 5th Guards Armoured Brigade was a component unit of the Guards Armoured Division while the 29th Armoured Brigade was an integral part of the 11th Armoured Division (7th Armoured Division's tank regiments used Cromwells along with Sherman Fireflies).

The other four (4th, 8th, 27th and 33rd Armoured Brigades) were independent brigades, assigned to Corps and divisional commanders as the need arose.

By 1943, all British armoured divisions were to have an armoured reconnaissance regiment normally provided with Cromwells since the Normandy landings, a new kind of unit which, sometimes, came to be used as a fourth tank battalion.

The British Army employed various types of the Sherman. Besides Fireflies, many of them were 75 mm tanks, like the M4 and the M4A1, the M4A2 and the M4A4. Usually, not all variants were represented in a single formation at the same time.

At the start of 1945, the 11th British Armoured Division gave up its Shermans, replacing them with the new A34 Comet heavy cruiser tanks. Canadian, Czechoslovakian and Polish armored units that fought in northwestern Europe were organized around the British pattern.

The 4th and 5th Canadian Armoured Divisions and the 1st and 2nd Canadian Armoured Brigades were completely equipped with Sherman tanks throughout the campaign in Europe, almost exclusively M4A2s, M4A4s and Fireflies. Contrary to what was expected, the armoured reconnaissance regiments of the two Canadian divisions operated Shermans and Stuarts instead of Cromwells.

The M4A4 and the Firefly were also the basic models allocated to the three armoured regiments in the 1st Polish Armoured Division. When the front stabilized near the Meuse, the majority of the tanks belonging to the 10th Polish Armoured Brigade were exchanged for brand new M4A1 (76) w Shermans. Trained by the British and deployed to France in late August 1944, the 1st Czechoslovak Independent Armoured Brigade was assigned to the role of containing the German garrison stationed at Dunkirk. The two (later three) battalion-sized tank regiments of the unit were basically outfitted with Cromwells but it is known that this brigade received three dozen Sherman Fireflies.

The technical disparity between the Sherman and last generation heavier German panzers did not have a significant impact on the course of the fighting. Other factors had a far greater importance than the technological balance between tanks.

One of the main reason was training: many inexperienced panzer crews were filling the enormous gaps caused by Germany's long years of war.

The Sherman had performed well due to the increasing quality of its crews and to new developed armor tactics: thanks to its superior mobility, the American medium tank was able to approach closely and hit the heavily armored panzers on thin sides where they could be easily penetrated. More reliable and more numerous than its adversaries, the Sherman certainly was good enough to prevail in the European Theater of Operations.

US ARMY SHERMANS

▲ Exhaust stacks and air intake vents being installed on a U.S. M4 (75) in England prior to D-Day. The tank was waterproofed using various sealing materials. US NARA

▼ Generals Eisenhower and Montgomery, as well as Air Chief Marshal Tedder, observing 3rd Armored Division's exercises alongside its commander, General Watson. The tank is a M4A1 (75) with one piece cast upper hull. UK, February 1944. US NARA

▲ A rare view of a M4 (75) small hatch 'composite' hull. This is a forward observer tank of the 499th Armored Field Artillery Battalion, 14th Armored Division, photographed in United States in January 1944. Only about 50 tanks of this type were built, with the combination of cast and welded upper hull sections. US NARA

▶ A 2nd Armored Division M4 (75) fitted with wading stacks being loaded onto a Landing Ship Tank bound for Normandy. England, 7 June 1944. US NARA

▲ DESTROYER, a Baldwin produced M4 (75) equipped with Culin cutter device to get through the thick Norman hedgerows, has overturned. Deaths and severe injuries frequently arose from such accidents. Canisy (Normandy), July 1944. US NARA

▼ A M4 (75) large hatch 'composite' hull with Douglas hedgerows cutter speeds past an abandoned German 88 mm gun on August 15, 1944. On this tank the upper front end consisted of a single armor steel casting that was mated to the remainder of the hull, made of rolled homogeneous plate. This was the most common variant of 'composite' hull Shermans. US NARA

▲ A cast hull M4A1 (76) w probably knocked out in Normandy during 'Operation Cobra'. On this variant the rounds were carried in water protected racks to prevent fires when the tank was hit. All Sherman designations that include a 'w' suffix indicate that the tank in question had wet ammunition stowage bins. US NARA

▼ An early production M4A1 (76) w of the 3rd U.S. Armored Division. Chenee (Belgium), 7 September 1944. US NARA

▲ FREEDOM'S-FORCE, a Baldwin produced M4 (75) of the 3rd U.S. Armored Division, shows the full complement of additional armor: cheek appliqué on turret and three plates welded to the hull sides, one to the left and two to the right (not visible) over the ammunition bins. Sloping armor plates in front of drivers' hoods are also visible. Spontin (Belgium), September 1944. US NARA

▼ This M4A1 (75) of the 756th Tank Battalion was photographed in Aix-en-Provence in August 1944. It sports a two-tone camouflage made of earth yellow large bands over the usual olive drab. US NARA

▲ One of the first M4A3 (75) w tanks employed by U.S. Army in France. The angle of upper hull front on this later version is now 47° compared to 56° on early Shermans. US NARA

▼ A U.S. M4 (75) put out of action by a direct hit in the fight for Luneville (south east of Nancy). The small size of the drivers' hatches of the early Shermans was reported to have caused a number of crew injuries during exits in emergency situations. Late September 1944. US NARA

▲ A M4 (75) of the 745th Tank Battalion still fitted with its rear wading trunk, advances into Aachen. October 15, 1944. US NARA

▼ An early M4A1 (75) with initial suspension bogies knocked out near La Salle (France), on 3 November 1944. US NARA

▲ Sand-bags were placed on the glacis of this 3rd Armored Division M4 (75) to improve protection against panzerfaust rockets. Appliqué armor was added on the hull sides of earlier Shermans for better protection of ammunition stowage racks during production or remanufacturing. Stolberg (Germany), 3 November 1944. US NARA

▲ A column of M4A3 (75) w of the 14th Armored Division near Cirey (France), 23 November 1944. Notice the large hull hatch on the nearest tank. The turret is equipped with the late model commander's cupola. US NARA

▼ Although it has been hit by an 88 mm gun, this M4A3E2 'Jumbo' of the 6th Armored Division wasn't destroyed. Morville-sur-Nied (France), 16 November 1944. US NARA

▲ One of the rare M4A1 (75) dry stowage cast hull exclusively produced by Pressed Steel. The hull had 'cast in appliqué' and large hatches. This M4A1 is an ex 'duplex drive' swimming tank. Photo probably taken in Luxembourg, Fall 1944. US NARA

▼) M4A3 (75) w tanks of the 14th Armored Division in Epfig (France), 11 December 1944. These Shermans have the late glacis pattern with 'outboard' lifting rings. US NARA

▲ Sherman tanks equipped with vertical volute spring suspensions (VVSS) often had floatation problems in muddy ground. A prominent Allied star is painted on the early three-piece differential cover of this M4 (75). Notice the added armor plates on turret cheek and drivers' hoods. US NARA

▲ This front view of a M4 (75) shows the two added frontal armor plates and the three-piece differential cover. US NARA

▲ A M4 (75) from C Company, 68th Tank Battalion, 6th Armored Division, maneuvers through muddy ground. US NARA

▲ Shermans with vertical volute spring suspensions (VVSS) were plagued by mobility problems on soft ground because the narrow tracks gave high ground pressure. As a stopgap solution, the Americans developed extended end connectors popularly called 'duck-bills' to add width to the tracks. US NARA

▼ Three Shermans and a M32 Armored Recovery Vehicle are pictured in Lemberg (France), 12 December 1944. The M4A3 (76) w in the foreground is followed by two M4A3 (75) w. These tanks of the 781st U.S. Tank Battalion are tied together to help pull a ditched Sherman not visible in photograph. US NARA

▲ A M4A3 (75) w of the 746th Tank Battalion with a set of corduroy matting on the hull front. These logs could be laid under the tracks if the mud became impassable. US NARA

▲ This M4A3 (76) w belonging to A Company, 48th Tank Battalion, 14th Armored Division, has added 'sand-bag armor' on the glacis. US NARA

▲ A camouflaged M4A1 (76) w of the 2nd Armored Division showing extensively worn off rubber chevron block tracks with 'duck-bill' extended end connectors. Frandeux (vicinity), Belgium, 27 December 1944. US NARA

▼ This picture shows COBRA KING, a 75 mm armed M4A3E2 of C Company, 37th Tank Battalion, 4th Armored Division, commanded by Lt. Charles P. Boggess that led the decisive final drive to relieve Bastogne. Notice the large writing on the hull. Bastogne (vicinity), Belgium, late December 1944. US NARA

▲ A M4 (75) of 4th Armored Division. Bastogne (vicinity), Belgium, 6 January 1945. US NARA

▲ This burned out M4 (75) 'composite' hull of the 6th Armored Division was knocked out near Wardin (Belgium) during the Battle of the Bulge. US NARA

▼ Wingen-sur-Moder, a small village located in northern Alsace (France), saw vicious fighting between American and German forces. This is a M4A3 (76) w of B Company, 781st U.S. Tank Battalion, photographed on 7 January 1945. US NARA

▲ German prisoners of war walk past a disabled American M4A3E2. Notice the thick gun mantlet of the tank. Foy (Belgium), January 1945. US NARA

▲ A crewman of the 10th Armored Division applies snow camouflage paint to his M4A3 (75) w. The 75 mm turret rear profile was raised a few inches to allow better clearance for the large drivers' hatches of the later hull Shermans. Belgium, January 1945. US NARA

▼ Lt. Col. Creighton Abrams, one of the top American tank aces of the war, commanded the 37th Tank Battalion of the 4th Armored Division during the Battle of the Bulge. He is seen here (on the right in the picture) near his M4A3 (76) w, named THUNDERBOLT VI, in January 1945. US NARA

▲ A whitewashed M4 (75) with extended end connectors pictured in a snow-covered field. Many 'duck-bills' were locally manufactured in France and Belgium. Ardennes, January 1945. US NARA

▼ A crewman loads ammunition into his M4A3 (105). This is an howitzer armed Sherman of the 48th Tank Battalion, 14th Armored Division, photographed near Hatten (Belgium) on 20 January 1945. US NARA

▲ A tanker of 42nd Tank Battalion, 11th Armored Division, mend his clothes on an old sewing machine in front of a M4A3 (75) w. Steinbach (Belgium), 23 January 1945. US NARA

▲ 75 mm Shermans could also be employed in supplementary artillery role. In this picture, M4A3 (75) w tanks serving with A Company, 23rd Tank Battalion, 12th Armored Division, provide indirect fire support to friendly units. Gambsheim (vicinity) France, January 1945. US NARA

▼ A heavily sand-bagged M4A3 (76) w of the 14th Armored Division seen in Niederbetsdorf (Alsace, France). Many tanks serving with U.S. Seventh Army units were fitted with a standardized kit consisting in metal cages welded to hulls and turrets to contain sand-bags as additional armor. US NARA

▲ After the Battle of the Bulge, the Americans began to add large armor plates to the glacis and turrets of various Sherman tanks. This up-armored M4A3 (76) w HVSS served with the 11th Armored Division. US NARA

▲ A thickly armored M4A3E2 'Jumbo' rearmed with a 76 mm gun. US NARA

▼ To permanently correct the floatation problem of the Sherman, the Americans developed new 23 inch wide tracks and horizontal volute spring suspensions (HVSS) that permitted to cross soft ground. This is a M4A3 (76) w HVSS of the 8th Armored Division with T66 steel tracks. Bocholtz (Holland), 23 February 1945. US NARA

▲ A M4A3 (76) w HVSS fitted with large additional armor on the hull front. Up-armored Shermans often led columns into areas defended by fierce anti-tank German units. US NARA

▲ This M4A3 (105) of the 10th Armored Division is seen towing the usual single axe ammunition trailer near Trier (Germany). Howitzer Shermans were used to provide indirect fire support to tank battalions. US NARA

▼ This M4A3 (75) w from the 5th Armored Division sports a large improvised rack on the back of its turret. The oval loader's hatch, a feature of all turrets with raised rear profile, is open. Lovenich (Germany), 27 February 1945. US NARA

▲ The 761st and the 784th Tank Battalions were two colored American armored formations employed in the European Theater of Operations. This is a M4A3 (76) w of the 784th Tank Battalion followed by a M4A3 (75) w of the same unit. US NARA

▲ This M4A3 (76) w served with the 761st Tank Battalion, the most decorated African-American armored formation of the war. US NARA

▼A U.S. M4A3 (75) w sporting bogies fitted with one of the less common spoked wheels type. US NARA

▲ A M4A1 (76) w serving with E Company, 32nd Armored Regiment, 3rd Armored Division, photographed in Cologne (Germany). The presence of extended fender attachments on the hull sides points to the strong possibility that this 76 mm Sherman was a remanufactured tank. US NARA

▲ Another M4A1 (76) w of the 32nd Armored Regiment, 3rd Armored Division, seen in the ruins of Cologne (Germany). One of the new T26E3 Pershing heavy tanks assigned to the same unit can be seen on the right in the picture. US NARA

▼ This M4A1 (75) of the 741st Tank Battalion, fitted with a hedgerow cutter since Normandy operations, exhibits appliqué armor plates on hull and turret. The vehicle has Sommerfeld matting to permit the attachment of foliage camouflage. It is equipped with rubber T51 tracks and 'duck-bills' for better performance on muddy ground. Dumpelfeld (Germany), 9 March 1943. US NARA

▲ In order to improve glacis armor, a number of tanks like this M4A3 (76) w were fitted with a layer of concrete. Gelsenkirchen (Germany), 19 March 1945. US NARA

▲ A knocked out early dry stowage M4A3 (75). It is a remanufactured Sherman with appliqué armor and extended fenders of the 745th U.S. Tank Battalion. Rottbitze (Germany), 20 March 1945. US NARA

▲ Shermans of 6th Armored Division move forward. The tank in the foreground is a radial-engine powered M4 (105). US NARA

▼ Front view of a large hatch hull M4A3 (75) w. This tank has T51 rubber block tracks fitted with 'duck-bills'. US NARA

▲ 'Duck-bill' extended end connectors broke off easily as seen on this M4 (75) of the 735th Tank Battalion. US NARA

▲ This M4A3 (75) w of the 9th Armored Division has the late glacis pattern with lifting rings in 'outboard' position. The late style 'sharp nose' one-piece differential cover is clearly evident. Westhausen (Germany), 10 April 1945. US NARA

▲ A M4A3 (76) w HVSS and a M4A1 (75) pictured in Nuremberg (Germany). US NARA

▼ The wreck of a very early M4A1 (75) lies in Nuremberg Stadium. This completely burned out tank has appliqué armor upgrades and cages to contain sand-bags as additional armor. The late commander cupola on the turret is noteworthy. Nuremberg (Germany), April 1945. US NARA

▲ An American M4A3 (75) w photographed in Leipzig (Germany). US NARA

▲ A remanufactured M4 (75) of the 20th Armored Division crosses the Danube on 27 April 1945. This tank, with riveted lower hull, was originally built by Pressed Steel and sports an unusual oversized appliqué armor on the hull. US NARA

▲ A M4A3 (76) w of the 12th U.S. Armored Division named WAS IST DAS (English translation: WHAT IS THIS). Notice the shape of the new enlarged turret that equipped all 76 mm Shermans. US NARA

▲ A M4 (75) of the U.S. 7th Armored Division gets its tracks wet in the Baltic Sea near Rehna (Germany), on 3 May 1945. US NARA

▼ A M4A3 (105) HVSS of the 13th Armored Division crosses the border between Germany and Austria. The name ANDY is barely visible on the right side of the turret. This tank has 23 inch wide rubber backed T80 metal tracks. US NARA

▲ Elements of U.S. 20th Armored Division first engaged the enemy near Dorf (Germany) on 25 April 1945. This picture shows a M4A3 (76) w HVSS of the unit in Salzburg (Austria). It is thought that a few radial engine M4 (105) HVSS had served with the 20th Armored Division in the closing days of the war. US NARA

▲ A large hatch hull M4A1 (76) w advances in Dobrany, Czechoslovakia, on 6 May 1945. Early production 76 mm Shermans can often be distinguished by the absence of muzzle brake on the gun US NARA

▲ A M4A3 (76) w HVSS of the 11th Armored Division fords the Muhl River. Neufelden (Austria), 4 May 1945. US NARA

▲ A M4A3 (76) w HVSS of the 37th Tank Battalion, 4th Armored Division, photographed in Czechoslovakia before the end of the war. Patton's Third Army liberated the western portion of the country. US NARA

▲ A M4A3 (75) w of the 16th Armored Division welcomed by local civilians and partisans rolls through Pilsen (Czechoslovakia) on 6 May 1945. There is photographic evidence that this division fielded some M4A3 (75) w equipped with horizontal volute spring suspensions (HVSS). US NARA

▲ This unique picture depicts a M4A1 (76) w HVSS serving with the 735th U.S. Tank Battalion. Even if the general consensus is that such tanks arrived too late in the theater, it's possible that this Sherman was delivered to the unit before the end of hostilities. Germany, Spring 1945. Private Collection

BRITISH SHERMANS

▲ The British adopted a different naming system for the Sherman. They used roman numerals past the tank's name to differentiate the various models. This picture shows a Sherman V (British designation for the 75 mm armed M4A4) of 79th British Armoured Division loaded into a landing craft. The hull is provided with direct vision slots installed in the driver's and assistant driver's hoods. The outer casting of the M34 gun mount (also known as rotor shield) is the older type without cast in 'wing' pieces. Ipswich (vicinity), England, 28 January 1944. Private Collection

▲ A Landing Craft Tank is being loaded with a Fisher built Sherman III (British designation for the 75 mm armed M4A2) of C Squadron, 13th/18th Hussars, 27th Armoured Brigade. Gosport (England), June 1944. Private Collection

▲ VIRGIN, a Sherman III of HQ, 8th Armoured Brigade, arrives in Normandy (France). Sherman IIIs were equipped with a General Motors diesel engine. US NARA

▲ The Firefly conversion was exclusively carried out on M4 (Sherman I), M4 'composite' (Sherman I 'hybrid') and M4A4 (Sherman V) tanks. British Firefly designations end with the letter 'c' that indicates the adoption of the 17-pdr gun. This picture shows a Sherman IC 'hybrid' in Normandy (France). US NARA

▼ A Sherman I 'hybrid' of 144th Royal Armoured Corps Regiment, 33rd Armoured Brigade. Author's collection

▲ FOX, a Sherman V of 'F' Battery, Royal Marines Armoured Support Group, photographed in Normandy (France) on 13 June 1944. White numbers and gradations are painted around the turret. In theory a crew member standing outside the turret could direct the tank fire by lining up the numbers to the target. Private collection

▲ This Sherman VC of 44th Royal Tank Regiment, 4th Armoured Brigade, has the rearmost sections of the sandshields welded to rear hull to stow additional equipment. It was a widespread practice, peculiar to this brigade. Normandy (France), June 1944. US NARA

▲ A Sherman III of 13th/18th Hussars, 27th Armoured Brigade. The brigade was broken up at the end of July 1944 because of casualties. The 13th/18th Hussars went to 8th Armoured Brigade, the East Riding Yeomanry to 33rd Armoured Brigade. The Staffordshire Yeomanry returned to England. Author's collection

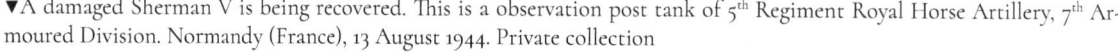

▲ A Sherman V Observation Post of HQ, 29th Armoured Brigade, 11th Armoured Division. This tank was the personal mount of Brigadier Roscoe Harvey (left), seen here with Major General George Roberts (right), commander of the Division. Normandy (France), Summer 1944. Private collection

▼A damaged Sherman V is being recovered. This is a observation post tank of 5th Regiment Royal Horse Artillery, 7th Armoured Division. Normandy (France), 13 August 1944. Private collection

▲ British tankers are loading 17-pounder ammunition into HANGING HOUGHTON, a Sherman VC of C Squadron, 1st Northamptonshire Yeomanry, 33rd Armoured Brigade. As other tanks of its Squadron, this Firefly was named after a village in the Daventry district of Northamptonshire Country. France, Summer 1944. Private collection

▲ Sherman V tanks of the 2nd Grenadier Guards, Guards Armoured Division move in Villers-Bretonneux, the small French town known for being the site of the first tank-versus-tank battle that took place on 24 April 1918. The Sherman Vs (Chrysler built M4A4s) were only produced with the 3-piece differential cover. Author's collection

▼ Tanks of B Squadron, 2nd Irish Guards, Guards Armoured Division cross the Waal road bridge in Nijmegen (Holland) during Operation 'Market Garden' on 21 September 1944. BUNCRANA, the Sherman VC in the foreground (probably named after a town in Donegal Country, Ireland) is followed by several Sherman Vs. US NARA

▲ A knocked out Sherman IC is inspected by a U.S. paratrooper. Notice the armor plate welded over the hull bow machine gun position. Fireflies had a 4 men crew because the assistant driver was eliminated in order to get more room for the 17-pdr ammunition. Erf (vicinity), Holland, September 1944. US NARA

▼ The British XXX Corps played a decisive role in the Battle of the Bulge, halting the German drive towards the river Meuse. Here, Shermans of the East Riding Yeomanry, 33rd Armoured Brigade line up in Hotton (Belgium) on 4 January 1945. The two tanks in the foreground are both Sherman ICs. Their long 17-pdr barrels are resting on the travel locks at the back of the hulls. US NARA

▲ SNOW WHITE, a Sherman V of HQ, 5th Guards Armoured Brigade, in Valkenswaard (Holland), on 17 September 1944. Author collection

▲ A Sherman II (British designation for the 75 mm armed M4A1) with thickened sides over sponson ammunition bins. This new hull design was introduced by Pressed Steel in October 1943. Private collection

▲ SHAGGY DOG, a Sherman III of C Squadron, 4th/7th Royal Dragoon Guards, 8th Armoured Brigade leads a British column through the Reichswald. Private Collection

▼ A destroyed Sherman II of Royal Scots Greys, 4th Armoured Brigade, lies in a field near Nederweert (Holland). The tank has a turret without the 'pistol port' on left side and is fitted with a 'cutter' device. Gemeentearchief Weert

▲ INDIANA, a Sherman I of B Squadron, 1st Northamptonshire Yeomanry, 33rd Armoured Brigade, moves near Udenhout (Holland) on 29 October 1944. Three months later, the Brigade was converted to Buffaloes in preparation for the Rhine crossing. Private Collection

▲ MARGARET, a Sherman II of 4th Armoured Brigade, pictured in the vicinity of Weert (Holland), on 26 September 1944. Gemeentearchief Weert

▼ LANCASHIRE, a Sherman III of 8th Armoured Brigade in Kevelaer (Germany) on 4 March 1945. Private Collection

▲ Sherman IIIs and Sherman VCs of 8th Armoured Brigade moving through Kevelaer (Germany), 4 March 1945. Private Collection

▲ A British Sherman IC 'hybrid' fitted with T48 rubber tracks and 'duck-bills'. Hamburg (Germany), 4 May 1945. Australian War Memorial

CANADIAN SHERMANS

▲ In order to obtain the necessary space for the installation of the exhaust wading stack, the large rear stowage box was moved slightly upwards from its original position on this Sherman VC of 2nd Canadian Armoured Brigade equipped with T62 steel tracks. The Canadian Army adopted the British classification system for the Sherman. Courseulles-sur-Mer (Normandy), June 1944. Library Archives Canada.

▲ CHASER, a Sherman VC of 27th Armoured Regiment (The Sherbrooke Fusiliers), 2nd Canadian Armoured Brigade, knocked out near Authie (Normandy) on 7 June 1944. The 17-pdr gun of the Firefly was always fitted on a standard 75 mm turret. This tank had a turret built without the 'pistol port'. Private collection

▼ Two Sherman IIIs of 10th Armoured Regiment (The Fort Garry Horse), 2nd Canadian Armoured Brigade destroyed in Rots (Normandy) on 11 June 1944. Sherman IIIs were the standard 75 mm gun tank for the 2nd Armoured Brigade, and were not used ordinarily by any other Canadian unit in Nortwestern Europe. Library Archives Canada

▲ A Canadian Sherman III of C Squadron, The Sherbrooke Fusiliers, moves through Caen (Normandy). Although not visible, the British stowage box fixed to the turret rear bears the tactical sign for the C Squadron (a dark colored circle with blue outline) and the individual number (14) in white paint. Library Archives Canada

▼ A Canadian Sherman V knocked out in Normandy. This tank served with the South Alberta Regiment, the reconnaissance unit of 4th Canadian Armoured Division. The fire burnt the rubber moulded around the right track blocks, only the metal skeleton remained intact. Private Collection

▲ A Sherman III from B Squadron, 27th Armoured Regiment (The Sherbrooke Fusiliers), 2nd Armoured Brigade, supports Canadian troops in a street of Falaise (Normandy), on 17 August 1944. This tank may well be BOMB, which is discussed further. Library Archives Canada

▲ A Sherman V from the 29th Armoured Reconnaissance Regiment (South Alberta). The tank's turret was up-armored with a track section taken from a German Panther. Bergen op Zoom (Holland), 29 October 1944. Library Archives Canada

▲ A Sherman VC followed by a Sherman IC. These Canadian Fireflies served with the Fort Garry Horse. Holland, 30 October 1944. Library Archives Canada

▼ Rear view of a Canadian Sherman VC in Leeuwarden (Holland), on 15 April 1945. The tank displays the markings of C Squadron, The Sherbrooke Fusiliers Regiment, 2nd Canadian Armoured Brigade. The quadrangular hatch over the gunner's position (left), a typical characteristic of Firefly turrets, is clearly visible. Private collection

▲ A Sherman V of 3rd Armoured Reconnaissance Regiment (General Governor's Horse Guards), 5th Canadian Armoured Division, covered with loads of track as extra armour. The extended mantlet of M34A1 Gun Mount protects both the telescopic sight and the coaxial machine gun. Library Archives Canada

▲ Another Canadian Firefly pictured in Leeuwarden (Holland). The 'low bustle' turret of this Sherman IC shows the 'cast in thickened cheek' on the right front and therefore lacks the 'pistol port' on the left side. Both the modifications were introduced at the same time. Private Collection

▼ A Sherman IC 'hybrid' of C Squadron, The Fort Garry Horse, passes infantrymen of Les Fusiliers Mont-Royal (2nd Canadian Infantry Division) near Munderloh (Germany), on 29 April 1945. Camouflage nets cover turret and hull sides. Library Archives Canada

▲ Sherman IB was the British designation for the M4 (105). The letter 'B' indicates the main armament, a U.S. M4 105 mm howitzer. This Sherman IB of 12th Canadian Armoured Regiment (Three Rivers Regiment), 1st Armoured Brigade, was pictured in Amsterdam (Holland) on 7 May 1945. Library Archives Canada

▲ AMI, a Sherman IB of A Squadron, Three Rivers Regiment, is inspected by local civilians during a parade. By March 1945, both the 1st Armoured Brigade and the 5th Armoured Division were transferred from Italy to Northwestern Europe where they fought till the end of hostilities. Holland, Spring 1945. Private Collection

▼ BOMB was the famous Sherman III of the Sherbrooke Fusiliers Regiment that landed in Normandy and remained in constant operation until the last day of war. It is seen here one year after its baptism of fire, as pointed out by the writing on the hull side: D+365. Zutphen (Holland), 8 June 1945. Library Archives Canada

CZECHOSLOVAK SHERMANS

▲ A Sherman IC of the 1st Armoured Regiment, 1st Czechoslovak Independent Armoured Brigade, pictured during operations against German units. The front half of the gun barrel is painted white in a wave pattern at the bottom, to make its length less conspicuous to enemy observers. Fireflies were primary targets of German anti-tank gunners. Dunkerque (France), April 1945. Private Collection

▼ Three Sherman IC 'hybrid' tanks of 2nd Armoured Regiment, 1st Czechoslovak Independent Armoured Brigade. Private Collection

FRENCH SHERMANS

▲ A M4A2 (75) of 2nd French Armored Division. The crew of this Sherman had probably fought in Tunisia on a French Somua S-35 tank as shown by the manufacturer's plate attached to the driver's hood. A paper with shipping data is taped on the assistant driver's hood. US NARA

▲ The Free French Forces established three Armored Divisions equipped with light and medium tanks supplied by United States. In this picture, TARENTAISE, a M4A2 (75) of 2ème Escadron, 12ème Régiment de Chasseurs d'Afrique, French 2nd Armored Division, is seen landing on Utah Beach (Normandy), 1 August 1944. This tank has an early production turret with lifting rings mounted in 'high' position. US NARA

▼ MOGHRANE, a M4 (105) from the same Escadron as TARENTAISE, arrives in Normandy. All 105 mm Shermans were produced with 47° large hatch hulls and high bustle turrets. The 2nd French Armored Division used a blue and white map of France with a Cross of Lorraine as formation insignia. US NARA

▲ M4A2 (75)s of 2nd French Armored Division await orders to move out for Paris. French tanks usually carried individual names. Crews serving with 12ème Régiment de Chasseurs d'Afrique favoured names of the old royal provinces (e.g. MAURIENNE, TARENTAISE). US NARA

▼ ST-QUENTIN, a M4A4 (75) of 4ème Escadron, 2ème Régiment de Cuirassiers, 1st French Armored Division, is pictured here in Marseille on 23 August 1944. The battle for the liberation of the town ended on 28 August 1944. US NARA

▲ US and Free French forces gave way to Operation Dragoon landings on the beaches of Southern France, on 15 August 1944. VALMY, a M4A4 (75) of 4ème Escadron, 2ème Régiment de Cuirassiers, 1st French Armored Division, is seen here heading to the front lines. It is equipped with T49 steel tracks. US NARA

▼ VESOUL, another M4A4 (75) from the same Escadron as VALMY and ST-QUENTIN, was also involved in operations against German troops in Marseille. All M4A4s were equipped with the bulky Chrysler A57 Multibank engine. The installation of the power plant requested the enlargement of the engine compartment, a modification that resulted in a lengthened hull. US NARA

▲ CHAMPAGNE, a M4A3 (76) w of 3ème Escadron, 12ème Régiment de Chasseurs d'Afrique, 2nd French Armored Division passes cheering civilians. This Sherman knocked out a German Panther in Place de la Concorde during the battle for Paris on 25 August 1944. US NARA

▼ M4 (105)s of 2nd Armored Division in Paris. 105mm Shermans weren't provided with 'wet ammunition stowage'. Of the 66 rounds, 45 were usually carried on the hull floor, 21 on armoured racks placed on the right sponson. Private Collection

▲ AUVERGNE, a M4A2 (75) of Groupement Tactique Langlade, 2nd French Armored Division in liberated Paris. The sharp corners and flat surfaces of welded drivers' hoods were exclusive characteristics of small hatch hull M4A2s produced at Fisher Tank Arsenal by late 1942. US NARA

▲ A M4A1 (75) of the 1er Régiment de Cuirassiers, 5th French Armored Division advances through a battered town. This division took part in the reduction of Colmar pocket and supported the French crossing of the Rhine in March 1945. Private collection

▼ MAROC, a M4A1 (76) w of 2éme Régiment de Chasseurs d'Afrique, 1st French Armored Division, crosses the Rhine. Altough some details are not visible, the tank certainly has a later style T23 turret with oval shaped loader's hatch and is equipped with T49 steel tracks and 'duck-bills'. Author collection

POLISH SHERMANS

▲ Formed on 26 February 1942, the 1st Polish Armoured Division (1 Dywizja Pancerna) played an important role in the liberation of France, Belgium and Holland. In Polish service, Shermans were usually identified with British designations. Here, a Sherman V of B Squadron, 1st Armoured Regiment, arrives in Arromanches. Normandy, late July 1944. Private Collection

▲ Two Sherman Vs of 24th Lancers Regiment (24 Pułk Ułanów), 10th Armoured Cavalry Brigade (10 Brygada Kawalerii Pancernej), 1st Polish Armoured Division. The larger spacing between the bogies than all other variants is one of the main recognition features of the Sherman V. Author collection

▼ A column of Sherman Vs from the 1st Polish Armoured Division in Normandy. All tanks have hull appliqué plates. Private collection

▲ Polish Sherman Vs prepare to cross the river Orne. Normandy, 8 August 1944. The 1st Armoured Division closed the corridor which was the only way out for the retreating German troops east of Argentan (Normandy) on 21st August. Library Archives Canada

▼ Sherman Vs from A Squadron, 24th Lancers Regiment cross the border between Belgium and Holland on 3 October 1944. Private Collection

▲ A Polish Sherman VC pictured in the Dutch town of Moerdijk on 10 November 1944. In Holland, Polish tanks were assisted by the sappers which ensured the crossing of numerous rivers and canals under heavy enemy fire. Author collection

▼ A Sherman IIA of B Squadron, 2nd Armoured Regiment (The British designation for the M4A1 (76) w was Sherman IIA. The letter 'A' indicated the U.S. 76 mm gun). Private collection

▲ Sherman IIAs of HQ, 2nd Armoured Regiment, 1st Polish Armoured Division pictured in Holland. The tank on the left, sporting a unique marking on the hull side, is the well known LATAJACA KROWA (translated from the Polish: Flying Cow), one of the most photographed Polish Shermans. Private collection

▼ Another Sherman IIA from the HQ, 2nd Armoured Regiment. The 1st Polish Armoured Division ended combat operations in Wilhelmshaven (Germany) on 5 May 1945. Private collection

BIBLIOGRAPHY

Books

- Chamberlain P., C. Ellis, *"British and American Tanks of World War II"*, ARCO Publishing Company, 1981.
- Culver B. *"Sherman in Action"*, Squadron/Signal Publications, 1977.
- Fletcher D., *"Sherman Firefly"*, Osprey Publishing Ltd., 2008.
- Forty G. *"United States Tanks of World War II"*, Blandford Press, 1989.
- Hunnicutt R.P., *"Sherman: A History of the American Medium Tank"*, Taurus Enterprises, 1978.
- Mesko J., *"Walk Around M4 Sherman"*, Squadron/Signal Publications, 2000.
- Sandars J. *"The Sherman Tank in British Service 1942-45"*, Osprey Publishing, 1982.
- Stansell P., Laughlin K., *"Son of Sherman Vol. 1: The Sherman Design and Development"*, The Ampersand Group, 2013.
- White B. T., *"British Tanks and Fighting Vehicles 1914-1945"* Ian Allan Ltd., 1970.
- Zaloga S. J., *"Armored Thunderbolt: The U.S. Army Sherman in World War II"*, Stackpole Books, 2008.
- Zaloga S. J., *"M4 (76mm) Sherman Medium Tank 1943-65"*, Osprey Publishing, 2003.
- Zaloga S. J., *"Patton's Tanks"*, Arms and Armour Press, 1984.
- Zaloga S. J., *"Sherman Medium Tank 1942-1945"*, Osprey Publishing, 1993.

U.S. Army Manuals

- Field Manual 17-12, *"Tank Gunnery"*, War Department, April 1943.
- Field Manual 17-30, *"Tank Platoon"*, War Department, October 1942.
- Field Manual 17-33, *"Tank Battalion"*, War Department, November 1944.
- Technical Manual 9-731 *"Medium Tank M4A2"*, War Department, January 1943.
- Technical Manual 9-731A, *"Medium Tanks M4 and M4A1"*, War Department, December 1942.
- Technical Manual 9-731AA, *"Medium Tank M4 (105 mm Howitzer) and Medium Tank M4A1 (76 mm Gun)"*, War Department, June 1944.
- Technical Manual 9-754, *"Medium Tank M4A4"*, War Department, January 1943.
- Technical Manual 9-759, *"Medium Tank M4A3"*, War Department, August 1942.
- Technical Manual 9-759, *"Medium Tank M4A3"*, War Department, September 1944.

TITOLI PUBBLICATI - ALREADY PUBLISHING

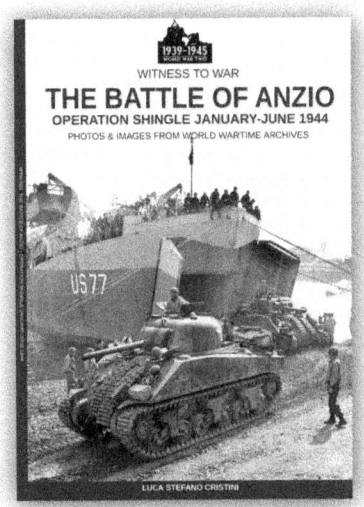

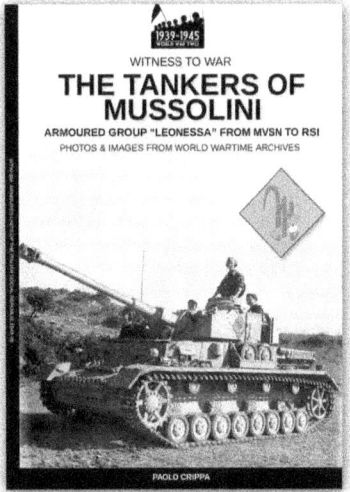
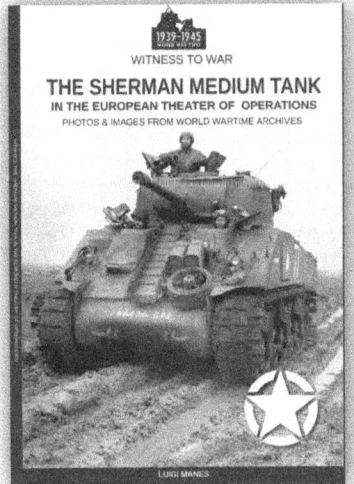

BOOKS TO COLLECT